MW00614551

THE
HIT

Despite the challenges that you have faced in life
and no matter how you feel, you are never alone!

TRAY WILLIAMS

The Hit
Despite the challenges that you have faced in life
and no matter how you feel, you are never alone!

Copyright © 2020 by Tray Williams

All rights are reserved solely by the author. The author guarantees
all contents are original and do not infringe upon the legal rights of
any other person or work. No part of this book has permission for
reproduction, stored in a retrieval system, or transmitted in any form
or by any means without expressed written consent of the author.

ISBN 978-0-578-86360-3

Scriptures marked KJV are taken from the King James Version (KJV)
Public Domain.

Scriptures marked NIV are taken from the Holy Bible, New International
Version®, NIV® Copyright ©1973, 1978, 1984, 2011 by Biblica, Inc.®
Used by permission. All rights are reserved worldwide.

Scriptures marked ESV from The Holy Bible, English Standard Version.
ESV® Text Edition: 2016. Copyright © 2001 by Crossway Bibles, a
publishing ministry of Good News Publishers.

Contents

Introduction

You might be asking, "Why would I want to read yet another book from yet another regular Joe?" Yeah, I am another regular man, but my story is far from ordinary. This trip down memory lane is full of traumatic moments, let downs, hiccups, aha moments, grinding times, mistakes, mistakes,and mistakes. What I have learned through every knockdown, either by my fault or not, not to wallow in it; yet, instead you should do like the American singer Aaliyah said in her song "Try Again:" that you need to "Dust yourself off and try again."

My name is Tray, and this book is dedicated to anyone who may be physically, mentally, or emotionally different from the next person. If you are, I am asking you to please not isolate yourself from others because of the insecurities about your differences. Because we truly do need each other to survive. There is absolutely no way I would still be alive and in my right mind today without the support of others. My uniquely-abled friends know that your life has purpose, potential, and you are loved.

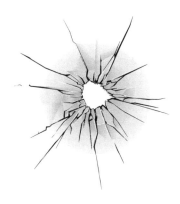

CHAPTER 1

The Good Ol' Days

Like any good story, the only appropriate way to start is, well, from the beginning. My beginning dates back to July 25, 1980 in Norfolk, Virginia. I come from a small, very tight-knit community

Growing up in Norfolk was short-lived, but we will get to that later. For the time being, I would like to tell you about how Norfolk treated me and my very small—but in my opinion, perfect—family. It was just my mom and my older sister, Tonya. I didn't have much of a relationship with my biological father, so my mother was the real deal, a superhero. In my youth, you could most certainly classify me as a mama's boy as we always remained close. There is also a two-year gap between my sister and me.

My sister and I were close, yet like every other sibling relationship on the planet, there was a significant amount of sibling rivalry between us. She, being the older girl, and me, being a boy and younger, caused a lot of conflict, but the disputes often resolved themselves at the end of the day.

I mainly spent my early toddler years in Virginia, but by the time I turned three, my family and I packed up and moved to Brunswick, Georgia, where we would spend the remainder of it. When I think back to my childhood years in Georgia, I remember when my mother and my former stepfather began to date. As a child, I, of course, had no sense as to what romance entailed. I just knew it was a man in my life, so I wanted to make the most of it while I could. One day, my mother, sister, and I took a trip in the car to the home of this mystery man.

"Mommy, where are we going?" I asked as I gazed out the back seat window.

"We are going to see someone very special to me, love." She looked in the rearview mirror as she responded.

Honestly, who could be that special to my mom, I thought. At three, I thought the only special people in my mother's life were Tonya and me, no one else, but I was wrong.

We pulled up to his mobile home. I remember the trees surrounding the area and the smell of the air, which seemed very different somehow. For some odd reason, this seemed like the beginning of something big. I hopped out of the car and approached the house on wheels,

How is this even possible? How can someone's house have wheels? Won't it just roll away, I thought. It baffled me, considering I had not seen anything like it before. My thoughts were interrupted by what sounded like a dog barking a few feet in front of me. We knocked on the old metal door that guarded my mother's lover's home.

"Hello, welcome. I've heard so much about you. It's a pleasure to meet you finally," the man spoke quietly to me.

I already don't like him.

I only thought like that because I had not had a relationship with my father; he never made it a priority to have me and Tonya in his life. The last thing I wanted was for a person to come into my life, make me feel secure, and then leave. That is why I have always looked at my mom in such a heroic way. She never left. She still cared for us, even when she felt alone at times.

After a few moments of me nervously talking myself out of the situation I currently was in, I shook the man's hand and greeted him politely with the manners my mom was teaching me. *I mean, this doesn't seem that bad.* Finally, I was greeted by the large Doberman I heard a few moments earlier outside the house. He was big, much larger than I was, but he was sweet and friendly from what I can recall. It was comforting to have the dog; it helped ease my discomfort in the situation.

By the time I turned four, my mother's relationship had progressed, and we began to plan the wedding ceremony. Still not understanding the big deal of romance, I partook and was named the honorary ring bearer. Honestly, the pressure was high. *What if I lose the rings on my way to deliver them?* Let's just say I didn't. What I did do, however, was rock my suit. It was a beautiful evening, even though I didn't see the significance of it.

After starting a life with this mystery man, I eventually learned how nice it was to have a male role model in my life. Looking back on my childhood, I, to a certain extent, felt what it was like to have a fatherly figure in my life despite the roller coaster the relationship would soon become. Eventually, he became physically and mentally abusive to my mom. It lasted until I got in high school when I grew close to his size and could defend my mother from his abuse.

To any man reading this book, there is never, ever, ever, ever any reason to hit a woman! If you do, you are weak and a punk. Be sure you will have to answer to God for hitting His daughter. Be afraid! Be very afraid!

Next, we packed up once again, and this time, we moved to Charlotte, North Carolina. I don't know exactly why Charlotte, but I truly loved it. It was all so fast. One minute it was just my mom, my sister, and I, and then the next, my stepdad joined the family and moved us to Charlotte. Granted, it took some adjusting to our new lifestyle. Deep down—I'm not sure why—as much as I wanted to have that security of the father figure in my life, I always thought I could still never have it.

As I continued through my early childhood, I wanted to clarify that there was one other very influential person in my life besides my mother. You see, it never occurred to me how vital this individual was until I got down to the nitty-gritty of writing my book. My grandfather was the only consistent man in my life when I didn't have a father to admire. He lived closed to me when we lived in Brunswick, GA. He trained me in a way that I still carry with me today. My grandfather bestowed such an integral personality. He was always so humble, and He was a shining example of a real man. I have always looked up to my grandfather, and I genuinely owe him my gratitude for becoming the man I am today.

Despite the inconsistencies in my life, God has blessed me with a few constants to guide me along the way.

Pause for Reflection...

Has there ever been a time in your life where you ever recall feeling so alone, borderline abandoned by someone or multiple individuals, where you felt should be there for your lifetime?

*What were your coping methods, positive and negative, knowing
that those people chose not to be there and that there was nothing
you could do to alter their decisions in staying or leaving?*

*Now, think of ways you can replace the negative with the positive
if that were to happen to you again.*

Moving on Up

Living in North Carolina, I met new friends that I would take with
me for years to come. In elementary school, I was very involved.
I loved math. It was my favorite subject out of all of them, so
sitting in class, I felt I had an advantage over the other students.
That was until the bell rang, and the teacher instructed us to
switch to English and Grammar. I'm not sure what it is about
this subject, but I have never liked it. I would even go a step
further and say that I hated it. Honestly, I still do—but that's
neither here nor there—and if you find any mistake while reading this, don't judge me! That's what makes the world colorful.
One person may be strong in writing, and another may be in
math. If it wasn't so, the world would be quite boring.

When I think back to the ages I was in grade school, I remember the teasing and bullying that came my way. More specifically,
my head has always been particularly larger than average, so it
was no surprise that the typical behavior kids exhibit would
lead me into the hands of the harsh words that came my way. Of
course, as a kid, it hit me a little more because all I wanted was
acceptance from my peers. My nickname that stuck throughout
elementary and middle school was "Big Head." *Wow, so creative.
They can't think of something better than that.* Deep down, I didn't
feel that way. It hurt, but I was always told by my mother and

grandfather that God made me special. At this point in my life, as I think back, I wish I hadn't taken those ignorant comments to heart because those kids did not know the real me nor took the time to.

I would be remiss if I did not take this opportunity to talk about the severity of bullying on maturing children. It is detrimental to their emotional health. I wish I had been given resources of people I could talk to or places I could go to when the bullying got to me. Therefore, I plead with you, if you or someone you know is going through bullying, seek help. First, lean onto God because He cares for you more than anyone. We are His children, and He loves us unconditionally (1 John 3:1). If you or someone you know needs additional help, please contact the Crisis and Suicide Hotline at (800) 273-8255. Support is there, and you can seek it. Be brave.

Most days, when I would come home from school, I would be greeted by the greatest companions. As a child, my family had several dogs. At one point, we had a Boston terrier named Beau. I didn't like Beau all that much, but my mother and Tonya seemed to like him. I just felt like he wasn't all that nice, and when I wanted to make time to play, he was more aggressive than anything else. He bit me several times, and it wasn't a play-play bite. I do remember one day coming home from school. It was an ordinary day.

"Mom, I'm home," I said from the open front door. "Come here, Beau."

Beau did not come because he had run away that day. As mean as that dog was, it still made me upset to know my pet had run away. Over time, my mom got another dog for us, Kim. Kim was a cocker spaniel, and this time we had a shot at having a good relationship. She was sweet and loving, and she enjoyed cuddling. We also had one more dog, and to be honest, I considered this dog my own. She was a Rottweiler, and her name was Jade.

After all the children ran to come home from a long day at school, we all piled outside to play at night—you know, back when the youth played outside. We found ourselves playing basketball, hide and seek (sometimes hide and kiss), kickball, "Mother May I," and "Simon Says." We would all hang out there for hours, the friends we made and the friends of friends. The most dreadful time would come when the sun would set, and we knew that we had to run our tails back home before those streetlights came on. The best days would have been during the summer, but once fall would come, we would have to turn back the clocks, which meant we received less time to play outside after school.

Now that I think about it, growing up, I didn't have that many friends because of the bullying and moving around a good bit. Of course, I had those who I would associate with in the school, but that was about it

My deepest fear was the thought of losing my mother. My mom was the type of person to make a really bad situation into an amazing memory. Despite our circumstances, she did her very best to provide a fair and healthy life for me and my sister, so losing her was always my greatest fear. Unfortunately, I lost her while writing this book.

Pause for Reflection

Read the second chapter of Second Kings.

Recall a time where you felt the love of a mother. Was it your own mother or a woman that took on the role to be there for you despite unforeseen events in your life?

We often have many maternal figures in our lives. Think of the maternal figures in your life and celebrate their life.

How does a love of a mother for her child compare to the love the Father has for us?

Before the Storm

By the time high school approached, things changed quite a bit for me. I gained confidence socially but got off a few exits early when it came to my academics. I never was really into homework. *If I have to spend almost ten hours in school five days a week, what is the point of homework?* I would think to myself.

I made a lot of friends. Now I was not a juvenile delinquent, but I did have my rebellious stage like every other teen. Most of my mischievous behavior happened when I had finally hit my teen years. My friends and I would go to our local convenience store after spending the afternoon and early evening playing basketball at the public basketball courts.

Upon entering the store, my stomach would growl uncontrollably at the smell of the delicious snacks and drinks. I remember hearing the soda and Icee machines roar as they produced more of the sugary drinks. The aisles flooded with the best snacks from chips to pastries to candies. My friends almost always would venture off to the back of the store to gather their food items.

My kleptomania began when a friend said, "Go ahead, Tray, no one is watching. Just grab one."

Despite my discomfort, I did. I knew that it was wrong, but let us be real here, after a long day of school and a night at the park playing an intense game of five on five, my thirteen-year-old self did not think clearly and grabbed the closest Snickers that was in my arms reach and stuffed it into the pockets of my ripped-up, red basketball shorts.

The walk home brought about a mixture of conflicting emotions. I felt the guilt of my behavior creep in, but at the same time, I was satisfied as I ripped open the chocolate bar. One Snickers eventually evolved into me going through strangers' cars and stealing money out of men's wallets that were left on the bleachers at the gym. God said in Galatians 5:9, "a little yeast leavens the whole loaf." This means one bad action can have a snowball effect and thereby cause a horrible habit. This bad habit led me to two trips to the police station and a 90-day probation in my first couple of years in high school.

CHAPTER 2

The Hit

"Humm-be, humm-bay, rockin' and rolling,' movin' and a-grooving," Coach Caldwell said at football practice the week before the first game of the year. That was his way of pepping us up after summer vacation. Mid whistle blow, Coach would yell. However, I was only thinking about two essential things: when this practice was going to be over and, more importantly, that pot of spaghetti my mom was making that night for dinner.

This was me as a hefty seventeen-year-old boy. I was a typical teenage boy, trying to find myself. I became fond of music, sports, lifting weights, and girls. However, there was not anything I was particularly good at doing. For most of my teen years, I became quite a jokester and gained the title of "Class Clown" for cracking ridiculous remarks to my mentors and quickly finding the humor in the most simplistic aspects of life.

It was the first week of my senior year of high school at Camden County High in Kingsland, Georgia. a small town where football rules and Friday nights light the town.

It was time for tackling drills, and I was up next. I hated this part of the practice. I was strong, but I could never get the right tackling technique down. Coach Caldwell blew the whistle, and my teammate and I ran full speed at each other.

What was the result of the collision? My teammate might as well have been a semitruck because he ran right over me. I was thinking to myself, *I'm not going out like no punk.*

"Coach, let's hit again," I said—well, at least in my mind, that's what I thought I was saying.

All that came out verbally was, "Uba, uba, uba."

As Coach Caldwell was talking to me, I repeated, "Uba, uba, uba."

At that point, I was like an infant—I began drooling. I was drooling uncontrollably. Little did I know, this would become a drooling complex that would stick with me for years. I also discovered I couldn't feel my right foot. I didn't know what to think at this point, and I thought it was bizarre I was experiencing all of these randomly. At this time in my life, I hadn't yet been exposed to the term stroke, nor did I have someone in my circle of influence that was a victim of one. So, of course, my mind was not there at all, thinking I could have potentially had one right in the middle of football practice. I was a teenage boy full of machismo, so I knew this was not going to keep me down. I would be back at practice tomorrow for sure, I thought.

Concern, more than shock, grew within me. Coach Caldwell told Eric, the water boy, to take me to the locker room and to call my mom. He didn't seem that concerned. I guess he just figured I was kind of dazed. I'm not sure if he even called my mom to check on me.

"Hello!" I heard her say.

"Uba, uba, uba," was all I could say.

I wasn't coherent enough to have a phone conversation, but I tried.

"Uba, uba," I repeated to my mom.

"What?" she shouted with frustration.

Looking around the locker room, I realized I was alone. Honestly, it felt okay being alone until a little later. The coach was still out on the field conducting practice, and the water boy had headed back out to the field as well. Frustrated, I just hung up the phone and decided I would attempt to drive myself home. I was frustrated and alone in that quiet, musty locker room, so I threw caution with the wind and left. Somehow, I was able to make my way out to my car. I swerved off the road a couple of times, but I made it safely home. Thank God for the rural town of St. Marys. There was never any real traffic.

I limped in the door, still drooling, though not as heavy as right after the hit at practice. As I walked through the foyer dragging my nearly numb leg, all I could think about was how tasty the spaghetti smelled.

As I entered the kitchen where mom was cooking, she immediately noticed something was seriously wrong with me. She turned that pot of spaghetti off, told my stepfather she was taking me to the emergency room, and rushed me out the door and into her car. My stepfather was recovering from hip surgery, so he stayed at home.

On the way to the emergency room, I was just thinking about getting back home to that pot of spaghetti. When we arrived at the emergency room, the nurses took one look at me and said I needed to have a CT scan. They instructed my mom to stay in the ER triage room while the nurses rolled me to radiology. They told her they would bring me back to that room once the CT scan was completed. I was just thinking, *Hurry up, so I can go home.*

A doctor came in to talk with my mom after they brought me back and said,

"Ms. Buckley, your son has had a stroke due to the fluid build-up on his brain caused by hydrocephalus. This is usually a condition that is diagnosed in infancy. Doctors measure the circumference of the baby's head, and if it's large enough they will take an x-ray of the brain." I don't know why the doctors didn't catch this when I was a baby because I always had a big head.

I had no idea what that meant. All I could think of was whether I would be out of the hospital by school tomorrow—and that pot of spaghetti waiting for me at home.

My speech had improved enough that I asked the doctor, "Am I gonna be able to go to school tomorrow?"

"No, we need to keep you for observation."

Not only did he keep me overnight for observation, but the doctor also sent me to Southeast Georgia Regional Hospital, a larger hospital in Brunswick, Georgia, for further tests. After a couple of days in the hospital, my teammates and great friends, Hiram Floyd and Boyd Way, came to visit me. They brought me a game-day polo shirt that all the team members wore on game day.

Many do not realize that generosity toward a person sticks with them for a lifetime.

I still remember when my teammates visited me like it was yesterday. That support is what I needed, considering I was still not educated on what was going on with my brain and my body.

Coach Caldwell also came to visit me, which meant a lot. I never blamed my coach for what happened to me. Back then, we were living in a different era of football. Toughness was required to be successful at the sport. Nothing ever dared to be said about brain injury during our time in the game or practices. If someone had cognitive impairments after a hit, we just said, "You got your clock cleaned."

I stayed there for about a week before the doctors in Brunswick concluded that the injuries warranted a surgical procedure on my brain to release the blockage of fluid within my brain. Since I was still legally a minor, I was transported to Scottish Rite Children's Hospital in Atlanta, Georgia. My mother was distraught, but I don't think my stepfather was too concerned. I was just worried about missing school. My mother and grandfather, who was my role model for how a real man should walk in life, drove me to Atlanta. The drive took us five hours to complete due to the location of where we lived at the time. All of this was very bizarre and new to me. It all happened so fast, so when my injury occurred so unexpectedly, it threw all of us off and hit hard considering my healthy childhood.

To be frank, I do not recall going to the doctor as a child, except for a minor case of pneumonia that I came down with when I was four. The day before the surgery, my mom and I stayed at the Ronald McDonald House. However, the night of my procedure, she remained in the hospital with me. I was extremely grateful they allowed her to do so. I needed her support. Brain surgery was a scary prospect! Like a little child, I wanted my mommy by my side.

Thankfully, the surgery was successful, and I remained in the hospital several days after for observational purposes. Every time the doctor had come to check on me, my question was the same: when was I getting out? Friday was the first football game of the year, I told him, and I wanted to be a part of it.

Early Friday morning, the doctors discharged me. On the way home, I didn't want to stop for lunch or anything. All I wanted was to make it back in time for the game. However, we did end up making a brief pitstop for some Kentucky Fried Chicken, but I could only eat a couple of bites because it took me a while to regain my appetite. When it came back, though, it came with a vengeance. I was amazed at how my mom could afford to feed me, considering my stomach was like a black hole. Her love and cooking were big parts of my recovery for the remainder of that year.

However, I did not know my mom had a differing view of me attending the game.

"Boy, you are crazy! You just had major surgery," she said. "And you're still drooling a lot. Maybe you can go to a game in a couple of weeks."

When we returned home from my stay at the hospital, my friend Latoya came over to help me plead with my mom about going to the season's opening game. Latoya told her that she would watch out for me, ultimately persuading my mom into agreeing to let me go.

My teammates crowded around but they were afraid to touch me. During the game, I carried a towel with me to catch the drool. I was able to stand on the sidelines with the team, which meant the world to me. I don't recall whether we won or not, but it meant a lot to look into the stands and see the crowd rooting us on.

For the rest of the season, I went to every practice and game unless I needed to be in Atlanta for a doctor's appointment. I was pretty much a glorified water boy; however, that did not matter to me. I was just pleased to be part of the team. In all honesty, it was much more difficult during the cold months to deal with the severe effects, especially my numb foot, which hung around somewhere between six and ten months. The team graciously voted me to be a co-captain of the team for that year. It was such an honor!

During the final game of the season, which also was Senior Night, I attempted to get Coach Caldwell to put me in for at least one play, just to down the ball. I knew there would be no tackling because the quarterback would drop to his knee, ending the game. Of course, Coach Caldwell would not allow it. However, he did let me dress in my football pads, helmet, and uniform. I have never seen myself any different than the next person. So, I always felt I could play, even with slurred speech and the side effects leaving me numb.

Grateful for the Simple Things

I always saw myself as a low-maintenance child until my teenage years when clothes and shoes either built or killed your reputation. After the stroke, I became extra grateful for the simple things that I overlooked and took for granted before that accident. I walked differently, I talked differently—heck, I ate a little bit differently because food would fall out of my mouth often, but I still was able to do mostly everything anyone else could do. Hence, the term uniquely-abled. All that said, I was just happy to be still alive, to be able to walk and talk, despite being a little impaired in comparison to others. I was most grateful that I was still able to eat my mom's fantastic cooking. I was very appreciative of Boyd Way, Sammie Stevens, Shawnta Jenkins, Sharica Simmons, Terrance Pelzer, and Sylvia Myers for still hanging out with me that year. They were my best friends in high school. I even had the honor of being a groomsman at Sammie and Shawnta's wedding a few years later.

Despite my impairments, I still had a fun senior year. I was able to go to all the senior events, such as graduation night at Disney World in Orlando, the senior prom, senior skip day, and the graduation party. I enjoyed riding to school with Sylvia and acting crazy. She was such a cool friend. I looked at Sylvia more like a guy friend, although she was lovely. We would stop and dance on the side of the road just to see the expression on people's faces. I would enjoy the dance but then walk around in pain afterward. Though my foot had minimal sensation, it felt like I was stuck with pins and needles. If you've ever had your foot or arm fall asleep, then you'll know how I felt, but in my case, it was all of the time.

I realized that even though I had some impairments, I still was physically and mentally able to do most things. It may always take me a little longer to do some tasks, but my best effort is enough in my sight and, most importantly, in God's sight (Col. 3:23). That's my message to anyone who is physically, mentally, or socially impaired. Your personal best effort is enough. Never let anyone look down on your best effort. As long as you are truly giving 100 percent, I believe God is proud of you. It is all a part of God's plan for your life (Ps. 139:14). There are not and will never be carbon copy people in this world. Your particular best is more than enough.

I wanted to take the opportunity at the life I had been given very seriously because it could have been a lot worse.

Ever since I was eight, I wanted to go to college, even though I never really gave one hundred percent effort in school. I would watch like Rodney Dangerfield's *Back to School*, and think, *I want to be there one day.* I gave one hundred percent in my weight training class but in my other courses, not so much. However, after my accident, I started giving 120 percent in all that I did, whether in school or at home. The way I saw it, my physical abilities were about 80 percent of a normal person's. Therefore, I believed that if I gave 120 percent in everything, I would catch up with everyone else. Even though I was giving my best now, I still worried about my potential acceptance to the college I wanted to attend. My grades from the first three years of high school were mediocre at best.

My mom's friend told her that if I read Psalm 34 every night before I went to bed, I would get into the college I wanted. So I did. Heck, what did I have to lose? That was the first time I opened the Bible my grandmother gave me for Christmas nine years earlier. Every night, I read Psalm 34 at least one time and said the Lord's Prayer, which my grandmother taught me when I was eight. I read Psalm 34 so much that I had the whole chapter memorized. Before this time, I thought being a Christian was something for older, married people. I thought I was only supposed to pray to Jesus when I needed something.

Psalm 34 awakened in me just how much God cared about me and all that was going on in my life.

That was the real beginning of my adulthood. I learned firsthand the Word of God doesn't come back void (Isa. 55:11). That one passage of scripture in the book of Psalm was all it took for God to start working on me. I still wasn't through with having fun and vulgar dancing at clubs and parties, or whatever I thought was fun, but that entire year, the Holy Spirit was speaking to me and working on me. Each night, as I read Psalm 34 right before going to bed, it filled my mind with God's powerful promises and truths.

However, I was still a young and foolish teenager. Even though my leg was fragile and I couldn't talk clearly, I always wanted to go to clubs and chase girls. Although I never caught the girls, I got a big A for effort. I remember being in the Paradome, a nightclub in Jacksonville, on New Year's Eve—don't ask me how I got in. At the stroke of midnight, the managers dropped one thousand dollars from the ceiling in one- and five-dollar bills. When I bent over to pick up some of the money, this dude elbowed me in my head right where the doctor had cut the incision into my skull for the surgery. It swelled up like a balloon because it was still tender. I immediately dropped the money I had in my hand and sat down for the rest of the night.

Though I should have learned my lesson right then and there, I still had some growing up to do. That was just one of the nonsensical things that I tended to do from time to time. I would ride a bike without a helmet even though I'd had brain surgery several months before and jump into the deep end of a pool despite my incapability to swim. As a teenage boy, you think you are invincible. Despite my injury, I still thought like the boy I was.

Although I enjoyed some nonsensical things, I hit the books hard in my senior year. I started to study. I wanted to get into college. I tried to act as healthy as I could. My injuries progressively improved as I continued to just do life. Gradually, my speech began to get a little clearer, and I progressively gained more sensation in my leg. Toward the end of the school year, I went back to flipping burgers at McDonald's. I had been working there for a year before I had the stroke but hadn't resumed working. With my stepdad not working, that extra income helped our family a lot.

Approximately one month after taking the SAT, I met with my guidance counselor to discuss my college aspirations. The physical therapy that I received after my stroke ended up building my confidence, and I told my guidance counselor that I wanted to major in physical therapy. This was a change from the business major I wanted to pursue previously. After looking at my grades and my SAT scores, she suggested I start at a two-year college and then transfer to a four-year university.

Well, one thing that stroke put in me was this underdog drive. This brought on pride in my abilities. I was always trying to prove that I was able to do what anybody can do. Before the stroke, my efforts were mediocre at best. This new drive motivated me to give it my all, but as I would find out, that could only take me just so far.

I selected Armstrong State University, which has since merged with Georgia Southern University. I applied, and sure enough, I got accepted! I started with some remedial courses, but nonetheless, I got in. I was even eligible for the HOPE scholarship, which was given to high school graduates who graduated with at least a 3.0 GPA. My tuition would be paid as long as I maintained the same in my college coursework. Yay! After the first year, though, I lost the scholarship because my grades dropped.

Pause for Reflection...

As you follow my life's journey, there will be events and circumstances that you may relate to where you are in your journey. Take a few moments at the end of each chapter and reflect on what you have read. I will offer some questions to get you started.

Do you remember what friends did for you during a time in your life when you really needed their support or encouragement?

As an adult, would you say friends are more loyal as adults or children?

Read Psalm 34.

What impacted you the most from this passage of scripture?

How has it helped you at this time in your life?

CHAPTER 3

The Drop Off

Starting college was an exciting time for me. My stepdad drove up with me to Armstrong State University. As we walked into my dorm room, my eyes filled with tears. Once we dropped off my belongings in the room, my stepdad took me to the Market Buffet. For me, this was like the last meal before lethal injection. I knew I would not get cooking like that in the school cafeteria, and I definitely believed that not having my mom's meals was the equivalent of death. The best way I can possibly describe the meal I devoured is that it reminded me of my mother's. Soul food is my favorite and puts me right back into the loving arms and comfort of my mom. In my most humble opinion, there will never be a cook better than my mom. Back then, I was two hundred pounds simply because my mom's cooking was like crack to me. I yearned for it.

My stepdad and I returned to my dorm room one last time before he left me to this new chapter in my life. Despite my stepfather's abuse to my mother, he was still the breadwinner in the family I still treated him with respect while he was in the picture. Once again, tears filled my eyes. *Alright, man up, dude,* I told myself. To be frank, I was extremely nervous and just a little bit scared. It was a new time in my life and the idea of not knowing what was coming terrified me. I had no idea the people I would eventually meet and how I assimilate to living away from my family and friends back at home, especially after my stroke. As I opened the door to what would be my home for the next four years of my life, a thought crossed my head: *What in the world? There are no pictures. There is nothing. This doesn't feel homey at all. I don't know if I can do this.* After my brief moment of doubt, I made it a priority to reassure myself that I would be okay. On that note, my roommate, Delvin, walked into the room a few moments after I did. Delvin was a cool, hardworking brother from Mobile, Alabama. He had a laid-back personality, was good with the ladies, and made them laugh a lot. We connected much faster than I did with my other roommates. One of the main reasons was that he was interested in similar activities as me—partying and girls—even though I never ended up getting the girls.

Also, Delvin and I would exercise together and eat in the cafeteria. I found that the dorm was set up apartment-style, except for the kitchen. The apartment that we were living in during our time enrolled at university had two rooms with two beds in each room, a common living room area, as well as a bathroom that divided up the two bedrooms. Think about it, four guys from different households sharing one bathroom—that was not the most sanitary place in the world, to say the least.

By placing four devout Christian girls in the room next to us, God was setting me up for "the fix."

The girls were Janie, Tonya, Anetta, and Sheila. We all got along well. We would watch movies and ate in the cafeteria together. Sylvia and Sharica, two of my best friends from high school, attended college here too. College didn't seem so bad after all. Even though I was there to obtain a degree, I wanted to chase girls and party. Deep down, I really didn't have peace.

What a Year!

After a Kappa fraternity party, the Christian girls invited me to their church at Overcoming By Faith Ministries. The pastor of the church was very charismatic and down to earth. I also noticed a youthful tone of those who attended.

He was similar to my grandfather who was also a pastor. He was always my role model for how to be a real man who loves his family and God and works hard.

The weekend of the Georgia Southern University football team's homecoming game in Statesboro, Delvin and I went together to the club. "Scrub the ground; let me hear you say scrub the ground." I was soaking wet with sweat from dancing in a provocative way. I would never say dancing is bad. I still like to dance even though I still have no rhythm whatsoever, but I now believe some things should not be done between two com-plete strangers. I felt something in my conscience say, "You asked God to give you your speech back; you asked Him to get you into the college you wanted to go to. He did that. Then you worried about how to pay for college. He helped you become eligible for the HOPE scholarship. Now, you're going to continue to do what you're doing to Him?"

My heart was broken as I realized what my lifestyle was doing to God after all He had done for me.

At that moment, I surrendered my life to Jesus. I didn't know what that meant. All I knew was that I was running from God and what I felt in my conscience for a year. Now, I had peace—real, lasting peace. The next morning, I got a speeding ticket as I was trying to get to church to make my salvation official, even though I didn't need to make it official. The minute I believed in my heart and confessed with my mouth, I was definitely saved.

If you declare with your mouth, Jesus is Lord,
and believe in your heart the God raised Him from the dead,
you will be saved. (Rom. 10:9)

Whoa! What a year it had been! I could hardly believe all that happened to me in that one short year! I went from being a class clown to a stroke survivor, to a college student, to a child of God. God said that what the devil meant for evil, God turned it around for my good (Gen. 50:20). It took another year for me to learn that I no longer had to do things alone. Before becoming a child of God, I had always lived by a mantra: if you worked hard for things, you would get good results. That is true to some extent. However, Jesus said, "Apart from Me you can do nothing" (John 15:5 NIV). Moreover in Luke 18:27, Jesus said, "What is impossible with man is possible with God" (NIV).

Now that I am His, He is always here to do life **with me** because He is **inside of me** (John 14:4-5). However, at the beginning of my walk with Jesus, that truth still hadn't registered with me yet, so God knew He had to make His love and mercy for me evident through the lives of other people I would soon come to know during my time away at university.

Finally, I learned that was the whole point of Jesus dying for our sins—because we can't live a perfect life or even a perfect day. That is why Jesus gave us the Holy Spirit. He told us the Holy Spirit would come to change us for the better, to remind us of what He said, and to help us go through life's ups and downs.

At that time, my whole goal was to prove myself capable because I had limitations in my speech and my mobility. I wanted to prove that I could do anything the next man or woman could do. I was driven by the need to prove to the world, or those that I thought were naysayers, that I was not disabled. Even though my foot was numb, I would quickly limp or jog around campus to prove that I could do it. I would study, study, study and not go anywhere on the weekend, trying to prove my mental ability. I hadn't yet come to the realization that with God, the only standard is Jesus. When God looks at us, he sees the cross, and we are all on level ground at the foot of it. There is no human standard. My standard is my individual absolute best effort.

----
*Trying to prove yourself can be good, but
you must have the right focus.*

My focus was on my abilities and what I could do, but I needed to focus on my abilities through Christ's strength (John 15:5). I remember studying through the night into the early morning for a pre-calculus test when I felt God urging me to ask Him for help. I stupidly said, *Hold up, God. In a minute. I'm busy...after I'm done.* I failed that test.

At the end of that year, I only had nine credits out of the thirty I attempted, the reason being that my high school did not prepare me for college. I didn't know the definition of studying. Unfortunately, due to this academic challenge, I lost the scholarship, and I had to turn to student loans. I get queasy just saying the words student loans.

I remember going home in between

the summer and the fall semester, nervous to come clean to my family about my college experience concerning my academics. Still, I told my stepfather about my grades.

"Maybe college is not for you. You should maybe do something else. I don't think you are cut out for this," my stepfather said as he looked me in my eyes on our living room sofa. My mom, on the other hand, was supportive like she always was.

His response offended me, and I said to myself, *You can doubt me, but don't you doubt my God.* Right then, my focus changed. I was now focused on God's ability, not my own.

I prayed to God a simple prayer: "I can't do this by myself, God. Please take the wheel, and I will be the copilot." During this time, I began to learn more about Jesus and His love for me. Then one morning, I read the ninth chapter of the Gospel of John, and my eyes teared up with joy.

Previously I had met a lady, one of those holy-roller, sin-sniffer types, who found out about my health issues and said to me, "You must have sin in your life."

I thought, *Am I being punished?* Then I read in this chapter where they thought the same thing about the blind man. Jesus said that no one had sinned, but his blindness was so God would get the glory. That was so liberating to me. That became a life verse and assured me that my mission was that God would receive glory from my impairment.

Never let anyone automatically insist that you are
going through a rough time because of sin.

Especially if they don't know anything about your daily habits. I don't make a habit of sinning, but I sin nonetheless. The Bible says, "There is none perfect, no not one" (Rom. 3:10-12). So that lady needed to do like the Michael Jackson song states: "I'm looking at the man in the mirror." There are indeed some natural consequences for our sins. For instance, if you were to steal a car, you will go to jail. However, God will help us get through those rough times as we repent and move forward (John 16:33).

From that moment until I finished graduate school, I earned mostly As and Bs with maybe two or three Cs along the way, the reason being that I started relying on God's ability and not my own. That relieved a lot of the pressure when I took my exams. All I needed to do was prepare the best I could and give it to God to do the rest. It's what Pastor Darren Bennett calls "Gospel Chill."

The irony here is that as the years continued, I began to allocate significantly less time to my studies and instead focused on extracurricular activities. Some of these activities came at random. but still had a positive impact on me and my social life. I was in gospel comedy plays, the Graduate Student Government Association, and even volunteered as the basket-ball team mascot.

I had great roommates during college: Delvin, Kevin, Jeff, and Tyrone. I even had the honor and blessing of being a groomsman at the weddings of Kevin and Jeff!

Understanding God's Unconditional Love

I went through a period where I was confused about God's love and how he poured it unto me. I got the purpose of fasting twisted. I was told fasting brings you closer to God, which I feel is true, but I was also told that you must deny your flesh. That was the part I got twisted. I recall a particular time whenever someone asked me to pray for them, and I assumed that I would need to do some kind of fast for time to prove that I loved God. Although I knew Jesus was the only way to gain salvation and enter Heaven, I still believed that I needed to prove to God, the Father, that I loved Him above all else, especially food because of its importance in my life. For Him to answer my prayer, I thought I had to sacrifice for it, like the Jews in the Old Testament. I decided that since I valued food so much, surely I needed to fast from it to cleanse my sin. From all that fasting, I lost twenty pounds, which was good, but I needed to learn an important truth about God's love. The truth is that Jesus is the only way to the Father, that when he died on the cross He paid it all.

Pastor Charles Roberson and Marty Youngblood lovingly mentored me through that period when I battled through finding the truth in God's unconditional love for me. They explained that there was absolutely nothing I could do that could make God love me any more or any less. Before, I thought His love was conditional. However, fasting didn't make Him love me any more than He did the night I gave Him my heart on that homecoming weekend. You see, when it comes to our Heavenly Father, you must not doubt or question whether you are worthy of his love and grace.

My undergraduate years started pretty healthy other than the lingering effects of the stroke. However, during my last two undergraduate semesters, I began to feel weak and fatigued. I didn't know what was wrong with me. When summer came, I went home to begin an internship helping to prepare meal plans for patients at the local hospital. However, I started losing the skin on my nose, and I was getting bald spots on my head, which concerned my mom. She thought I should sit out for a semester.

With my mom's input and wisdom under consideration, I still leaned onto God and prayed and sought His direction. God confirmed I was to return to school to earn a Master of Public Health. *Huh, I haven't finished my bachelor's yet,* I thought. Yet, I remembered God knows the end before the beginning (Rom. 4:17), so I decided to follow God's plan.

When I went back to school, I was still having health problems. I was going to a minimum of two or three doctor appointments per week, trying to determine what was going on with me. Test after test, x-ray after x-ray, biopsy after biopsy, including a biopsy of my lip as well as one of my bone marrow. They just couldn't find out what was wrong with me. Thank God I had completed my coursework. I just had to finish my research paper from my summer internship and go to my work-study job. which I had for most of my undergraduate years.

That last semester of my undergraduate degree, I worked for the computer science department, where I met a wonderful coworker and outstanding person who became a great friend, Allyson. She was a graduate assistant, and she would cover for me at my job if I needed to go to the doctor.

After two months with that schedule of two to three doctor appointments a week, I finally had an endoscopy procedure scheduled for the morning. I had gotten used to all the tests, so I just thought this would just be a normal day. Little did I know there would be a lot more action that day. When I came home after the test, I ate a bowl of cereal because I was feeling weak. It was extremely cold, and although it was October in Savannah, the weather was still warm. I began to shiver until I could barely breathe.

I called Jeff, my former roommate and great friend, and asked him to take me to the emergency room. We went to Memorial Health Hospital, where my doctor was, which was clear across town. I was in line to register in the emergency room, and when I eventually approached the receptionist, she saw me shaking so much that she called the triage nurse to take me back to a room. After they took my bloodwork, I was admitted. My white and red blood counts were just too low to release me. As a result, I spent the next two weeks in the hospital as the doctors tried to figure out what was wrong with me. The doctors called my mom and explained everything to her. She was worried. It had to be like déjà vu to her: her only son in the hospital, just four years removed from being the first person in the family to have a stroke.

One day, I developed masses on the bottom of my feet that were so big that it hurt to walk. My friend Don stayed overnight with me to help me when I needed to walk around my hospital room. The doctors did a biopsy of the masses and were able to pinpoint the problem: systemic lupus.

"Lupus? What is that?" my mom asked the doctors.

I had never heard of lupus, just like I had never heard of or been exposed to anyone that had suffered from strokes in the past, but I soon learned that lupus is an autoimmune disease in which your immune system attacks your body. The doctors put me on an aggressive treatment of prednisone, a steroid (rat poison, I call it), and two immunosuppressant medications. When on prednisone, it became difficult for me to sleep, and I became even hungrier than before. From then on, I was always cold, which aggravated lupus. Warm soup and hot baths were my gifts from God (James 1:17).

At that point, my condition was so active, I couldn't stay alone and I had several doctor appointments in the coming week. I couldn't go home because my mom lived an hour and a half from the college. Do you remember that I said Ally was an outstanding person? She and her new husband, Olli, invited me to stay with them. They let me take unlimited baths at their house. Due to my condition, I would even take baths in the middle of the night because I was always cold.

I still needed my family's care for my long-term health, so I decided to go home to my mom. I went home for the rest of that semester and finished my graduation paper. My mom lovingly took care of me during that time. She would check in on me, and she also cooked those wonderful meals that only she could do. I was torn between being home in a house with family or being in my dorm room around many friends for my recovery.

I had my desktop computer with some AOL trial disks. Back then, homes with internet access were not as common as they are today. These disks provided thirty days of free dial-up internet access. I needed the internet because I needed to do the research for my graduation research paper,

I would work for an hour and then lay down. For you young people, dial-up internet is like watching grass grow. This was no such high-speed internet in homes at that time, or at least it was not common. I did that for about a month until I finished my paper. After I emailed the final copy to my professor, I was approved for graduation. That physical trial of extreme weakness and insomnia took a toll on me. A major thing that impacted me during my time back at home during recovery was the fear that I would stop breathing while I was asleep at night, but Jesus would calm me down and rock me to sleep. Trust me, just tell him your concern, and he will give you that rest. He promised he would.

Come to me, all you who are weary and burdened, a nd I will give you rest. (Matt. 11:28)

In Jesus, there is always hope (Rom. 5:8).

Finally, the day of my graduation had come, but I was still feeling sick and weak. It was the month of December, and the cold outside was beating me up. The young lady next to me had prayed that I would soon be able to walk across the stage, despite my weakness. Finally, my name was called, and I walked across the stage. The president of Student Affairs, Joe Buck, hugged me because he knew of the battle I had endured. I received my diploma and pointed up to the sky because only Jesus made that happen.

Pause for Reflection...

You may relate to some of these events and circumstances. Take a few moments to pause and reflect on what you have read. Read these key lessons I have learned and answer these questions to get you started and then add your own thoughts.

My heart was broken as I realized what my lifestyle was doing to God after all He had done for me.

God said that what the devil meant for evil, God turned it around for my good (Gen. 50). That year was an example of that amazing truth about God.

Has anything happened in your life that is an example of this amazing love?

Trying to prove yourself can be good, but you must have the right focus.

What did I discover I needed to focus on instead of my abilities and what I could do?

Will you say the simple prayer I did so God can redirect your focus?

"I can't do this by myself, God. Please take the wheel, and I will be the copilot."

Review the scriptures mentioned in this chapter and record what you learn from each one.

Romans 10:9

Genesis 50:20

John 15:5

Luke 18:27

John 14:4-5

John 15:5

Romans 4:17

James 1:17

CHAPTER 4

It's Not Over; It's Just Beginning

I went home for the spring and summer to recover and reha-
bilitate. That was a tough time for me because I have always
been somebody who didn't like to stay in the house. I couldn't
drive because the hydroxychloroquine (rat poison) would give
me muscle spasms, so I stayed in the house most of the time. It
was horrible, I tell you.

God has not given us the spirit of fear. Yet, we get it sometimes, but He understands. We just need to let Him know, and
He will provide us with that peace, just like He did for me then
and still does today, if I were to be a little scaredy-cat.

> They that wait on the Lord shall
> renew their strength. (Isa. 40:31)

By the middle of the semester, I began to feel a lot stronger. I
remembered God imparting to me that I needed to get my Master

of Public Health. I didn't have all the answers of how or why I was going to do it, but I just trusted in His plan. It was similar to Abraham and Isaac. Abraham was told to go and kill his son. He didn't know all the details. Still, he was obedient, and God supplied another option.

In the same way. I knew God would supply the ability to complete my degree. So that fall, I went back to school to pursue my master's degree, despite the advice I had received. This was what I felt God was showing me He wanted me to accomplish next. It may have seemed foolish because of how I felt physically, but God uses those foolish things to accomplish His purposes (1 Cor. 1:27). That's what I would tell anyone: if you are sure that God has pressed on you to do something, I say go for it. He just sometimes doesn't think like us with our finite mind. Don't get me wrong, you definitely want to seek counsel, but if God honestly won't give you rest concerning it, go for it. It may not have seemed logical to some for me to go. God's logic is often not like our logic.

I was then diagnosed Aplastic Anemia (low blood counts) which was caused by the lupus because it can affect every system in your body. The doctors considered doing a bone marrow transplant, but they felt it was too risky with my overall condition. They decided to monitor me and said that I would be okay as long as I didn't start getting multiple infections. Since that time, you can ask anyone in my circle of friends who have known me for years, I have not even caught a cold or the flu, even though I have very low blood counts. That also isn't logical, but then again, God's ability isn't always understandable, but I'm thankful for it. Yay!

Pause for Reflection...
Read Isaiah 41

Do you recall a time where you struggled with the plot of your life?

If you acquire conflicting emotions and self-doubt,
What did you do to reassure yourself that God was in control?
remember it is God who will guide you all your life.

Now, given that I was a survivor of stroke, I decided to acquire more knowledge on such episodes to prevent a future one. Most of my research project was centered around the traumatic injury of strokes. When a person experiences a stroke, it is not merely a moment in time; rather it is life-changing. When an individual begins to experience it, they start to feel helpless. Some of the physical effects are guaranteed to make people feel self-conscious, almost as if they are an alien to onlookers. A person may walk differently or talk differently, leading people to look at or treat you differently. However, the closer I grew toward God, the more I realized that it didn't matter what people I don't know, think about how I look as far as my impairments.

At the end of the day, it only matters what God thinks. As long as He and I know that what I am doing is truly my best effort, that is more than enough for God. In other words, as long as I am doing the best I can with the hand I am dealt each day, that's OK. As with anybody with a chronic illness, some days I feel like I'm on cloud nine, and then the next day I feel like a train has run right over me and that I am not sure how exactly I will even get out of bed that morning to take care of my responsibilities. Whatever hand you are playing each day, just do your best, and I can promise you that will always be alright with God.

For those of you out there reading this book, whether you are uniquely-abled" or just insecure about your looks, you are great and marvelous just the way you are—no need for facelifts, nose jobs, bleached skin, or any other physical change to be a child of God. As long as you know you are doing your best (i.e., exercising, educating yourself, loving others), there is no reason to feel the need to alter who you are. You see, society has a great way of providing false illusions as to who you need to be and the standards you must meet, but God has made you the way you are now, in a way as intentional as anything else, because you are just that special to Him (Psalm 139:14). You are always on God's mind. There is not a day that goes by that he does long to be with you. Like that 1987 hit "Two Occasions," God only thinks about you on two occasions: day and night. Think about it. If I gave you the choice of two cars, would you want a basic, factory-made, silver Ford Focus or a black, tinted-window Tesla with all the bells and whistles? Come on, you and I both know that in this scenario, most people would choose the Tesla because it's different and stands out. That's you! You're different, and you stand out! That's great; God used special intention in making you and has a special purpose for your life.

It makes me think of a story of a young man who was an applicant for a once-in-a-lifetime job opportunity. He would have to make it through three rounds of interviews to get the position. What he didn't know is that the hiring manager already wanted him for the position after previously meeting him at an event and knowing his qualifications. His friend told him that the manager liked his male employees to have bald heads. so he cut his hair. Then after the second round of interviews, his other friend told him that the manager liked his male employees to wear a tie, so he wore a tie to the last interview with the hiring manager. At the end of the interview, the manager offered him the position. He happily accepted it, but then the manager said, "Let me ask you a question. Why did you cut your hair?" He then added, "You didn't need to wear a tie. I had already chosen you for this position." Be who God made you be and no one else.

Pause for Reflection...
Read Galatians 1:10.

Do you recall a time in your life where you unknowingly sought out the approval of man to feel worthy?

What did you feel in the aftermath?

Never seek out the approval of another person but only the acceptance of the Father.

I did pretty well as I completed my graduate coursework. Then, it was time for my practicum research project. This was a research project in which you perform a study at a local public health agency. I went to the stroke department at Memorial Health Hospital, which honestly was a shot in the dark, to see if I could do my research there. I was able to contact Brenda Krokoski, RN, BSN, who was the stroke department manager for all patients who came into the hospital with a stroke.

She took a chance on me and let me do my research project by interning with stroke patients in the hospital. She just has a heart for stroke survivors and will do anything to help them. I was such a unique case because of my age. I was a peer educator. I educated the stroke survivors in the hospital about symptoms of strokes and tested them on their ability to retain the knowledge after a stroke. It hit home in many ways and had many positives and negatives. Some good parts of my internship were that I was able to educate people on the illness that I battled and motivate them to overcome their adversity as I had mine. A negative was that it did bring up very real and scary memories from my past.

This was a wonderful time in my education because Brenda took me under her wing and taught me all about strokes and the brain. What a blessing! I even got to observe a stint being put in a patient's brain. I loved my research so much that I would even go into the hospital on my off days.

My new knowledge helped with my graduate presentation, which Brenda attended. She approved of my presentation, which I had been preparing for and gathering research for all of that semester. It was beyond exciting when I saw that I had completed all the requirements for it and had the opportunity to share all of my findings with the woman who mentored me and so graciously allowed me to shadow her for my research.

This not only was a great learning opportunity but a chance for me to test my boundaries and delve into new passions. Given this opportunity, I found myself even more thankful to medical professionals, who devote years to educating themselves on how to help people in need and dedicate the rest of their lives to that career path to execute it.

Brenda liked my presentation very much, so much, in fact, that she said if she got a contract with the hospital to get them certified under the Joint Commission on Accreditation of Healthcare Organization (JCAHO) in the future, she would have me come and speak.

Putting My Knowledge to Work

A couple of months before graduation, Tonya, a wonderful and loving sister at Kingdom Life Christian Fellowship, the church I attended my entire time in college. put in a good word for me at her job at Union Mission, Inc. because I finished all my requirements. Union Mission, Inc. is a homeless organization that provides healthcare and substance abuse programs to the homeless population in Savannah. I interviewed to be a Chronic Disease Prevention Coordinator and got the job! I was a novice in nonprofit work and implementing grants. Of course, I did what anyone would do in my position—I faked it until I made it.

I was providing preventative health education and health screenings for all the homeless in Savannah. I loved that job because I could use music and humor to relay a critical message to the less fortunate. I would act out the song as it played and tie the message of the song to healthy behaviors. I could just be myself, act silly, and get paid for it. Now, when I think about it, what can be better than that? Over the next two and a half years that followed, I grew in my wisdom, knowledge, and experience. I truly enjoyed every minute of it.

Seeds Planted

A while later, Brenda kept her word. She got a contract at Alta Bates Summit Hospital in Berkeley, California and was having a mini-conference for doctors and nurses on proper stroke care. I flew to the Bay Area for a week to give presentations at several locations. This experience was great for me, and I was able to discuss the importance of the topic and grow in my confidence. Previously, in 2000, I prayed that I would be able to fly across the country and speak on stroke prevention. News flash: God accepts small and big prayers; it does not matter the weight or cost of what is being prayed about but the content of your heart. If it's in His plan or His will, He not only can make it happen but will make it happen. Now, on the other hand, if a prayer goes unanswered, it might not necessarily be unanswered by God himself. Sometimes a His silence is an answer. Sometimes, God will tell us "not now" instead of "no" because He knows what will be best for us.

Five years later, it happened! Not only was I speaking to between one and two hundred nurses and doctors at one time, but I felt the most real love and confirmation from my Heavenly Father. It was in that moment where I thought, *Thank you so much, Jesus. Who am I to ever doubt your unconditional love?* You may think, what's the big deal about this, but to see faith in a goal you couldn't yet see come true brings out my emotions.

> Faith is the substance of things hoped for,
> the evidence of things not seen. (Heb. 11:1)

Furthermore, I will be forever grateful to Brenda for her dedication and drive in helping me make all this happen—well, that and the many other things she did for me. She also opened her home to me for a week when I graduated from college while I looked for work.

After that trip to Berkeley, I was hungry to live in a diverse area such as California because I had always had a craving for diversity. I started looking for jobs in California. My search went on for another six months until I finally found a position as the Director of Cultural Health Initiatives for Northern and Central Florida for the American Heart Association (AHA) in Jacksonville, Florida. This was not the geographical area I wanted to live in, especially with California's diverse culture and scenic mountains to compare, but I wanted to work for the AHA and would have the opportunity to speak on strokes. I decided to take what came my way and rolled with it because I knew to trust God and to lean on him during this new chapter in my life. I knew that God would protect me and guide me. He opened the doors to this new job opportunity and possibly closed other doors. I just had to take this opportunity. An added bonus was that I would actually be closer to family who lived directly across the border in Georgia.

I knew that the job was far from where I wanted to be in California and was above my experience qualifications, yet it was time to fake it until I make it. I was ready to begin the next phase of my life's journey.

Pause for Reflection...

This was a very trying time in my journey, but I learned a lot about being patient and seeking God's way rather than my own.

Have you experienced a trying year where you wondered how you were going to get through it?

Has my story encouraged you not to give up?

Take a few moments and reflect on the scripture referenced in this chapter. Add any insights or thoughts God reveals to you from each one. You may want to memorize the ones that make an impact on you and where you are in your journey right now.

Deuteronomy 31:6

Isaiah 40:31

1 Corinthians 1:27

Matthew 19:23-30

Hebrews 11:1

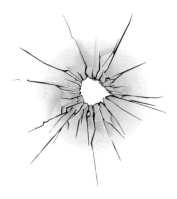

CHAPTER 5

Faking It Until I Make It

I was excited about starting my career with the AHA. It was a great-paying job with a lot of perks. I had desired to work for AHA ever since I volunteered at the yearly Heart Walk at Lake Mayer Park in Savannah.

With my newly acquired position at AHA, I flew up to Atlanta for orientation at the Marietta Greater Southeast Affiliate corporate office. This was such a bittersweet moment for me. As soon as I walked into the office, I saw familiar faces from the Heart Walk in Savannah. I was able to see Maritza Licameli, my vice president and supervisor, who valued my passion for stroke prevention over my lack of experience when choosing me for this position. I still have a warm place in my heart for her.

Remember how important it is to take chances and risks in life. You never know who is watching and the potential benefits that could come with it. Have faith!

I then went back to Jacksonville to try to fill some huge shoes because the previous director did an outstanding job. My coverage area was from Pensacola to Orlando, a large portion of the state of Florida. I would organize community events to educate about stroke and heart disease prevention, but my main job was to set up collaborations and partnerships with organizations like Historically Black Colleges and Universities, area hospitals, and churches. I loved speaking and giving presentations on stroke prevention and my story throughout Northern/Central Florida and Memphis TN, but trying to sell our programs with nothing tangible to offer was a daunting task for me.

The first three months were great, as I was learning the position and traveling a good bit. I loved the people I worked with in the office and in the community, where I did outreach work. Yet soon, I would find out that our lives are like the stock market—they have high peaks and sudden dips, and we don't always get a warning before the dips. At first, I was on a peak, but a sudden dip came upon me quickly. I was given a "Power to End Stroke" project to implement in Jacksonville's churches, but I felt I had bitten off more than I could chew. My quota of participants to sign on for the "Power to End Stroke" program, which promoted exercise and stroke awareness, was a constant stressor during that time. This meant more marketing meetings and more urgent emails in the middle of the night. I collaborated with Baptist Health Hospital for this event, which had a high quota and a deadline.

Well, Jesus said, "In this world, you will have trouble, but don't worry, I have overcome the world" (John 16:32-33). While trying to keep my head above water, I had taken my eyes off that. I was just trying to meet my goals, so I was going through the motions. There was a two-month period in which I didn't have a single day off.

As we got closer to the deadline, I started taking extreme heat from the local office's vice president. I wasn't meeting the quota, and needless to say, she was not a fan of mine. You could cut the tension in the office with a knife. There were cold stares that she would give me when I would greet her in the morning. Her almost daily inquiries concerning meeting the goals of the partnership even caused a shouting match one day. Well, it wasn't much of a match; she raised her voice while I listened. Anyone who knows me would know that I am a soft-spoken, mild-mannered person. I don't do that shouting thing. I already had more bags than a Publix supermarket under my eyes. Now, I had potato sacks under them because I couldn't sleep a wink. I was also sick from lupus, but I didn't have time to go to the doctor. So I had to be quiet about my health with anyone because I didn't want anyone to worry.

You would think from my previous life lesson in college, I would have known to put God first.

My mom would always say, "A hard head makes a soft behind." Again, I was stiff-arming God by not asking for His help and guidance. That was my mistake. At this time, I was also dating and actually became engaged to a young lady. That is right. Me, the pigeon-toed soldier, was engaged to be married. The only thing was, God clearly showed me she wasn't the one for me, and I needed to stop leading her on. She was an amazing woman but we ultimately weren't meant for each other, and I knew it. It was a huge age gap. She was 39 years old, and I was only 28 years old. Every night for a week, I would wake up at about two in the morning, and the first thing I would hear is, "She is not the one for you." I wouldn't be able to go back to sleep for the rest of the night. The headaches became so great, I walked around in a drunken stupor for lack of sleep.

I had to drive to meetings in Orlando and Daytona. Gas prices jumped to four dollars a gallon, and I didn't have enough money to put jelly on toast. Things got so bad that there were a couple times that I had to go cash my checks in advance at those rip-off places. One night, I didn't have anything in my cabinet but a can of tuna fish and a can of sweet peas, so I made a bowl of tuna fish soup. I want to throw up just thinking about it.

Finally, after much wrestling, I was obedient to God. I broke off the engagement, and then things started coming together. I started sleeping well again, my health improved, and I was able meet my quota. By this time, the tension in the office had resolved itself. I exceeded the goal, which made the vice president look good and satisfied with the collaboration, so she stopped being so cold toward me.

Then comes the 2008 recession. We received emails about coworkers across the southeast whose positions were downsized due to budget cuts. Thankfully, my name was not on that list, so I figured I was doing something right.

Things were going pretty well. I stayed in Riverside, a nice part of town, and I almost finished paying off my car. Things were looking up. However, sudden drops were soon to come.

One day in the office, my Blackberry rang. It was Maritza. She told me that she needed to come down to meet with me the next day. My heart dropped; I knew something was wrong. I got weak in the knees. Maritza never just came down without previous notice. I didn't sleep much that night. The next day, when she came into the office, she didn't wait to tell me why she had come so unexpectedly.

I approached her desk with the utmost fear in my heart as my eyes locked with hers. My stomach sank as the inevitable happened.

"Tray, because of budget cuts, your position was downsized. Don't finish what you are doing. Get your stuff together and go home. You will be given a small severance package."

She had tears in her eyes, so I understood she had to feel conflicted about letting me go.

When I got home, I felt like a boxer who had just been hit in the nose. I was dazed. *I moved down here for this job. What am I supposed to do now?* I wondered. I prayed all night.

When adversity occurs in life, don't break

Well, I had a good friend, Hopie, from Kingdom Life in Savannah, who lived in Ft. Lauderdale. I figured I would visit her for the weekend and then come back to Jacksonville to look for a job.

The next morning, I quickly packed and then headed south on I-95. This was my first time there—well, kind of. I had come to Ft. Lauderdale for half a day to sit on a stroke panel at the downtown Marriott.

Hopie had a one-bedroom apartment located on Davie Boulevard and I-95. I bunked on the couch. She, like me, had a heart for the homeless. She would hand out food to the homeless in Holiday Park every morning at nine, so we did that together. This helped me take my mind off my work situation. Twice a week, Hopie also made sack lunches for about seven men who lived under the I-95 overpass. This was great! I love spreading God's love like peanut butter.

When I accompanied her, one of the homeless guys stared at me.

He then said, "You look familiar."

"You do too," I said.

"Have you ever lived in Savannah?" he asked.

"Yes."

"Then, have you ever worked for a company called Union Mission?"

"Yes," I said again.

When he said, "Tray," the light bulb turned on in my memory. He was one of the guys I educated at a Savannah shelter. That blew my mind. I know it's a small world, but seven or eight hours away? One of the seven guys I fed was someone I knew. I was bewildered. I don't believe in coincidence; God knew that was going to happen before I was born (Jer. 1:5).

I asked God what just happened with the homeless guy. There was a reason for that happening. On my way back to Jacksonville, I began asking God about what happened. I felt Him say, clear in my spirit, "Forsake all and follow Me" (Luke 14:33). Well, I didn't have any ties to Jacksonville—I was only there a year—so I packed up my stuff, put it in storage, got out of my lease, and left to make a fresh start in South Florida. I looked foolish in the eyes of most people. I was living in a lovely home, I had family members close by, and the cost of living is lower in Jacksonville. But this move is what I had peace about with God. I didn't know all the details, like where I was going to live or when I was going to find a job, but similar to Abraham, I just knew God said, "Go." (Gen. 12:1). I would like to say that when coincidences happen in life, you may need to ask God why it happened and see what He says. It may not be as extreme as my case, but he may be trying to tell you something.

I slept on Hopie's couch for a month while I searched for a job. I had my little severance package that would help for about two months. I applied for unemployment. I had education and experience, so I thought, *I will find a job in no time.* Do you know that saying: "As a man thinketh, so is he?" In this case, wrong, wrong, wrong!   55

It was time for me to find a room to rent. Hopie had been so graceful to let me sleep on her couch, but a man needs to have his own place. I looked at several rooms within my price range, which was very little, considering I didn't have a job. I figured I would have a job within one or two months. Sometimes, I don't make choices with the best counsel; I've made them based on my wants. An example of that was about to occur in my life.

One of the places I looked to rent was in a house with three ladies, one of whom was very attractive. The place was across the street from a cemetery. God tells us to acknowledge Him in all our ways, and He will direct our paths (Prov. 3:6), so I knew to ask God. To tell you the truth, though, I asked Him which place would be best to rent, but it was one of those quick prayers aimed at the choice I wanted. I felt God steering me away from this place with the ladies, but I found a way to rationalize the choice nonetheless. Nothing was going on, but it wasn't the best choice when trying to hold out for a rib. I thought that the attractive lady could be my rib (wife), but needless to say, I thought wrong. I thought that attractive lady could be her, but needless to say, I thought wrong.

However, this choice of renting there sent me into a four-month hurricane of chaos. My car engine's pistons started knocking, signaling that the engine was pretty much done. My severance money ran out, and my roommate's dogs would relieve themselves on the couch. That being said, I never sat on that couch. I was forced to become familiar with Broward County Transit. The homeowner sometimes wouldn't pay the electric or water bill, so I would come home to complete darkness until he paid the bill. Sometimes, I couldn't take showers in the morning because the water was turned off. Then he would do something with the meter and turn it back on. So, South Florida heat combined with riding the bus, and no shower can produce an interesting odor. I also didn't find a job in my field. I remember sleeping on the floor because the room I rented didn't have a bed. Tears of brokenness rolled down my cheeks as I grieved about my situation.

My family urged me to come home but I felt that would have signified that I lacked faith. When I say I ran out of money, I mean it. I was brick broke. I didn't have $1.50 to catch the bus to church, so I walked the seven miles between my door and its front steps. By the time I got there, I was soaking wet with sweat from the intense heat of summer in South Florida. I probably smelled like a wet dog., but I needed to be around people.

Yes, through Jesus, we have forgiveness for our disobedience, but sometimes there are natural consequences to our disobedience. I was experiencing one of those consequences. I must say, though, as bad as it was, it wasn't all gloom and doom. Monique, my former coworker who I met in Memphis, TN, lived just fifteen minutes away from the room I boarded, so I would volunteer for her and spoke on my experience with stroke at numerous churches and community organizations in Palm Beach County. She would pick me up and bring leftovers and hot food for me to have a good meal. She would also have me over for dinners with her family. I still call her mom my "ma." In fact, one of Monique's volunteers told me about Calvary Chapel. I had never heard of that church, and I was kind of wary about it because the name sounded dry and boring, but one Sunday, I took a shot at it.

When I walked into the sanctuary, my eyes got big, like a kid in a candy store. There were all these cultures together.

"Wow!" I said, "That is how it is going to be in Heaven!"

The message was great as well. This instantly became home for me.

I looked to get plugged in right away; due to Jacksonville's isolation and the beating I took in the aftermath, I knew that friendships was highly needed. There was a men's Bible study on Tuesday mornings at seven, so I woke up early and went. I sat at the same table with a now good comrade of mine, Damon Penn, or D-lovish as I call him. Damon is definitely an extrovert; he immediately introduced himself to me and inquired about my situation. We actually used to go to the same club in Jacksonville, Cool Runnings, at the same time. He then lined me up with Matthew McFarlin, or MC, who was at the table with us as well. MC would become to me like what Jonathan was to David in the Bible, my best friend. He told me about the Rangers of Christ (ROC), a men's Bible study that met Mondays at seven in the evening, so I started going to that. I met some brothers there who truly had my back.

When I truly acknowledged God in all my ways, He faithfully made my path straight!

Pause for Reflection...

As you followed my journey in this chapter, you may have related to how I decided to try and do things on my own and therefore suffered the consequences of those decisions.

You would think from my previous lesson in college, I would have known to put God first, but as you read, I did not.

Have you also had these moments where you forget what God has taught you about listening to His still, small voice and then obeying it?

God was faithful despite my disobedience. Studying these scriptures helped me get back on the right track. Record how they help you and memorize the ones that you need for right now in your journey.

John 16:32-33

Isaiah 55:8-9

Jeremiah 1:5

Luke 14:33

Proverbs 3:6

CHAPTER 6

No Notice at All

One day, I got back to the house after a regular day of catching the bus downtown to meet Hopie to feed the homeless at Holiday Park. After I finished, I took the bus back home to get dressed in my business casual attire to go apply for jobs. Ramon Hunley from ROC invited me to a Labor Day family barbecue at his house during this time. I was surprised he invited me to the family gathering at his place because he didn't know me well. Still to this day, ten years after, he and Debbie, his wife, never fail to invite me to whatever family gathering they have at their house, along with Daryl and Tasha Byrd, Akee, and Lisa Campbell; we all just do life together. They are my true family.

When I got home after the barbecue, Michelle, the head roommate, said, "The owner sold the house, and we have a week to find a place to live."

What now, God?, You got jokes. This ain't funny

I had gone through my small severance package. My unemployment check would not come for another two weeks, and I had no family I could stay with. All I had was a little more knowledge of the area, but of course, the only places I could afford were in the rough neighborhoods.

At the end of the week, I received another week's reprieve when the home buyer agreed to pay for hotel rooms for the three of us for a week. For me, that hotel was Extended Stay Embassy Suites, which was like living in a single-family home, considering where I was coming from.

That week, I diligently looked for places to stay and counted my blessings. Because at the end of the day I had a roof over my head. One of the places I looked at was with an older woman who kept her place exceptionally clean. I decided home was probably my best choice. However, God always knows what is best for us. When He says no or puts obstacles in our way, He may be protecting us from something harmful. God once again, intervened and used Damon Penn in this situation to keep me from staying at a place in a rough neighborhood.

Damon checked in with me to see how my search was going. I told him about my choice. He didn't like the neighborhood I was considering. He then said, "Let me ask around." He also announced my need at ROC and asked if anybody knew of any-thing to let me know. John Chambers (JC) was a brother who went to ROC. He had previously given me a ride to church when he saw me walking. It blew my mind that he would give a ride to someone he did not know. That just doesn't happen in South Florida. I thanked him and told him I was amazed that he had helped me.

John said something that still sticks with me to this day: "That's agape love, unconditional love."

The following Monday, after Damon made that announcement, John approached me. He said he had talked to his wife, Debbie, and they would let me stay at their two-bedroom duplex near the beach with them and their two boys, Sammie, who was one, and Joey, who was four-years-old, for one week. Again, I was astonished! John barely knew me, and Debbie didn't know me at all. Of course, I took this opportunity and happily stayed with them as I continued to look for new housing and job.

I remembered God's promise in Philippians 4:19,
"My God shall supply all your needs."

After breakfast, I would catch the bus looking for a job and a place to live during the day. That was a full traveling day on the bus for sure. Damon mentioned that there was a brother who had a room to rent available for $500 a month. The brother was Luis Gonzalez, who was from Peru. His other roommate was Rene Staeldi, a man from Switzerland. The room had a TV and a bed. I took the room and ran with it. I lived there for the next four years. Despite my best effort, I still did not find a job for two years!

Pause for Reflection...
Read Jeremiah 29:11.

What are some troubling times you have experienced in the past? Do you remember the hurdles you hit and had to overcome?

Who did you lean on during that time? Where did you develop in your faith to press into the Lord?

God says to us that all of his promises are "yes" and "amen". God knew—no, He planned for me to go through adversity before I even knew what was going on, but sure enough, He provided. When I was down in the dumps, He never let a day go by where all my needs was not met. Yes, I know I should never doubt God, but that was exactly what I did when the going got hard.

That room I was provided with was pretty much heaven compared to the last place I rented. Rene and Luis were both good people who loved God, so that was a plus. Luis and I would eat bootleg oatmeal. Bootleg oatmeal was gluten-free bread—regular bread for Luis— soaked in milk with a banana and blueberries and then microwaved. This dish was like food for my soul, a culinary delight.

Luis was a jack-of-all-trades type of fella who could fix anything, and he loved cycling. He would wake up early in the morning to go riding before the traffic got heavy. Thus, I gave him the nickname JP: *J* was for Jack-of-all-trades, and *P* was for a pedal. During my first year there, I couldn't drive because of my car's engine, so I would ride Rene's bike to get groceries and things.

One day, Rashad Shaheed, a man from ROC, came to pick me up to go to an event. That was the first time we got to know each other. He, MC, and I got along really well, so we started hanging out and soon became best friends. I like to think of us more like brothers. We hung out all the time, especially on the weekend. During the day, we would help move single mothers with ROC. At night, we would go to a concert, have a game night, or go to the movies. Rashad and I slept many nights on MC's living room floor. We were both looking for full-time jobs, even though Rashad did substitute teach from time to time. We would pour out our hearts to each other all the time.

Rashad and I both worked for the 2010 Census Bureau. I had never been so hated by everyone until those four months of the census. No one liked someone knocking at their door and asking for personal information. I had doors slammed in my face, and I had unanswered knocks in the heat of the summer. It was very humbling, but you do what you need to do to put food on the table. The good thing about it was that it extended my weeks of unemployment compensation. During this time, my mom and stepfather were without a stable home themselves, so I couldn't go home if I wanted to. My mom didn't have anywhere for me stay. I could've stayed with my grandparents, but there wasn't a lot of job opportunities for me there. So I felt I needed to stand firm.

Despite the challenges that came with being unemployed, a lot of great things happened to me during that time. MC, Rashad, Ramon, Daryl, and I were truly like blood brothers. Every holiday, we were at each other's houses, even eating Christmas and Thanksgiving dinners together. Their families adopted me into their own. God was truly supplying my physical, spiritual, and emo-tional needs despite the challenges of being unemployed.

Pause for Reflection...

As you followed my life's journey in this chapter, you may have related to how God showed His love and provision through so many people in my life. When I asked one of them why he was helping me, he said:

That's agape love, unconditional love.

What did you learn about showing unconditional love to others through these men and women of God who helped me through these difficult situations in my life?

Despite the challenges that came with being unemployed, a lot of great things happened to me during that time.

Are you experiencing challenges in your life?

What are some specific ways that your own friends and family have helped you?

Instead of focusing on the negative things that are happening, what are some of the great things that are happening to you?

Read Philippians 4:19.

Why does Paul say God will do this for the Philippians?

What did you see my friends do for me?

Look for ways you can help others and be God's hands in the community.

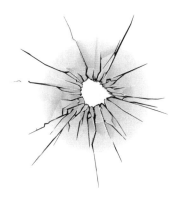

CHAPTER 7

The Ride

Another one of my weekly activities was volunteering at Calvary Chapel's service to the homeless. This was so dear to me for eight years. We would have a church service outside under tents and then feed them a complete meal with all the fixings. I met so many beautiful people who would become like family to me. Rain, sleet, or shine, we were out there loving on our guests.

After two years of being unemployed or underemployed, I had a strong desire to go on a mission trip. Despite my financial and professional challenges, I still wanted to participate and serve.

Sometimes, I feel you just need to make a move in faith.

The Mission Trip

When Calvary put out the list of the 2011 short-term mission trips, Nicaragua sparked my interest. I looked at my current situation. I didn't have enough money to put butter on toast. I was somewhat physically challenged, and I had many food intolerances. It was a perfect time to sign up for a mission trip, right? Well, to me it was. That way, if I could pay for the trip, physically keep up with the rest of the team, and not get sick, I could only give credit to God. After praying about it, I signed up. Once Calvary approved me to take the trip, I had to pay two thousand dollars, along with a twenty-dollar registration fee. I sent out an email to all my close friends, and within a matter of a week, I had the other $1,880.

Jym Kay was our trip leader. He was a great leader! One thing that stood out about him was his consistency. His personality and demeanor at six in the morning were the same at nine at night, even though we all worked hard all day. He was very loving and down to earth to everyone. We landed in Managua, the capital of Nicaragua.

As soon as we hit the ground, We went to a mission camp that provided support for the community, especially the youth. The camp was there to support the community. Despite the language barrier, I still hit it off with the teenage boys at the camp. We even had a special handshake.

One thing we did broke my heart. We went to a landfill where families had to live. They put up makeshift shelters and dressed in the discarded things they found. They would dig through the trash to collect the soda cans to sell and then purchase small amounts of food. When you go on a mission trip, you realize how blessed you are. Compared to this, what I was dealing with in the US was nothing. It put everything in perspective for all of us. When we returned stateside, the first thing I wanted to do was take a hot shower. That's one thing we take for granted: running hot water. On most, if not all, mission trips, you just have to rough it and take cold showers, if you even have running water available.

God's Delay Is Often His Blessing

Upon returning from the trip, I realized that I was still without a job and my unemployment compensation was almost expired. October of the previous year, I had gone to a job fair. It was there that I left my resume with a human resources representative of the AIDS Healthcare Foundation.[1] Every week after the fair, I would do a follow-up call to ask about the position. I was finally able to get through to the head HR person, and he had me meet with Eric Boyd, the program manager. It was a quick, laid-back interview in the Ross Dress for Less parking lot because the medical van was doing HIV testing there. I was offered a position. Yay! I truly appreciated that because in the two years I was unem-ployed, I had a few interviews I know I was qualified for and gave

[1] AIDS Healthcare Foundation (AHF) is a Los Angeles-based, global, nonprofit provider of HIV prevention services, testing, and health-care. AHF currently provides medical care and services to more than six-hundred-thousand individuals in fifteen US states and thirty-six countries worldwide.

good answers to the interview questions. However, I believe my physical difference caused them to decide not to hire me. Of course, they wouldn't flat out tell me that that was the reason, but I like to assume it was. I mean, hey, what do I know? I'm doing the best with what I have. Here is my suggestion to anyone who is uniquely-abled. Don't let other people's opinions affect a goal or dream God has put inside you. Don't lose heart. Go for it! God and His abilities are with you (Eph. 4:5).

Mr. Boyd told me that the only position available was a per-diem testing position on the mobile testing van, so whether I worked and got paid was to be determined on a day-to-day, as-needed basis. I applied for a hire level position based on my qualifications. Yet, beggars can't be choosers. I needed a job, so of course I took the position. I figured if I could get my foot in the door, I could move up in six months. There were only five of us on the team, so Mr. Boyd called me every day for the next two weeks. That was cool with me because I had plenty of days off over the prior two years of unemployment. I needed to work as much as I could to get used to working. After those two weeks, Mr. Boyd asked me to come on full time.

At that point, I realized God's delay can sometimes actually be a blessing.

I knew that if I'd found this full-time position earlier, I would not have been able to go on the mission trip, which was a lifelong dream of mine. God also knew I needed to acclimate back into the workforce before working a full schedule. Those are just a couple of examples that show how God strategically plans our lives with our good in mind. He continuously showed me He would provide what I needed when I needed it if I trust Him.

That first year on that job with the AIDS Healthcare Foundation was cool. Mr. Boyd was the coolest boss east of the Mississippi River. He went from being my boss to being my true big brother. I gave him a nickname, Dr. EB. His wife, Nadine, and his daughter, Asha, were part of the team also. They helped me so much.

The Ride

I have always loved to exercise. I believe the consistency I have created with staying active has helped me deal with some of the physical limitations I experienced from the stroke and lupus. From time to time, I would go on long-distance bike rides, sometimes as long as thirty or thirty-five miles, trying to be like JP (Luis). I would usually ride north on A1A along the beach, but after a while, I got bored with that path. So I mapped out a bike lane route going west on Commercial Boulevard. I wanted to ride early, so I got up at four thirty in the morning. I was on the road by five fifteen. There was no way I could know I would never be the same because what was about to happen during this ride. Everything started well. Of course, it was still dark. I remember riding past BJ's Wholesale Club, but my memory is blank after that point.

Pause for Reflection...

As you followed my life's journey in this chapter, you may have related to how I learned that God's delays can be blessings in disguise.

I know that if I'd found a full-time position any earlier, I would not have been able to go on the mission trip, a lifelong dream of mine. God strategically orchestrates our lives with our good in mind.

How has God shown you this to be true in your life?
Sometimes, I feel you just need to make a move in faith. Despite my financial and professional challenges, I still wanted to go on a mission trip. When I looked at my current situation, it could have discouraged me from taking that step in faith. However, as I did my part, God did His.

Is there something God is asking you to do that you do not feel you can do because of your current situation?

Read Philippians 4:18-19.

What is the key to receiving this amazing promise from God?

CHAPTER 8

The Room

I woke up with Rashad sitting in a chair right beside my hospital bed. Things were not clear to me. It was like I was daydreaming. I thought Rashad and I were in my old apartment in Savannah, but then I heard the nurses talking about my clinical notes. I knew something was not quite right.

I tried to ask Rashad, "Where are we?"

He must have understood what I was trying to ask, though I was finding it very difficult to speak with a tube down my throat. I was surprised by his answer.

"You're in the hospital. You were in a bicycle accident. "What!" I motioned. They found you on the side of the road," he told me. "You've been in an induced coma for three weeks. "How?" Your lost control, and you flipped over your handlebars and hit the concrete. Your head swelled to the size of a watermelon. You were unrecognizeable. You broke your Whawtoo."

Despite his explanation, it still didn't hit home. My mom and my sister had come down to the hospital during the first week after the accident, but they had to go back to work. Over the next three or four days, I was in and out of a fog. It was like I was daydreaming and couldn't focus on what was going on around me. It was kind of zombie-like. I guess that was due to all drugs they were using to ease my pain.

Since I had broken my jaw, the doctors had to wire it shut. My roommate, Joe, Rashad, and a couple of other brothers talked about how they brought pictures in so that the surgeon could know how I looked before the accident; that way, he would be able to make me look how I had once I could have some reconstructive surgery. The fellas were joking about how they had brought in a picture of a woman for the doctor to use, and in my drugged state, I thought they were serious. They got a big laugh over it, but I did not find it funny at all. I thought I had no control over what the doctors did while I was unconscious. I remember how Monique, Dominique (her daughter), and Ma (her mother) had visited me until midnight the night before the surgery. I couldn't sleep because I seriously thought the surgeons were going to change my physical identity, so for the next few days after the surgery, I thought I looked like a woman. I was scared to death by this. I was not amused in any way by their jokes. I thought the physical therapists was teaching me how to be a girl. All due respect ladies, I hated it.

I was not clear about everything that had happened. I only understood bits and pieces of what was going on. I remember praying to God, saying that I didn't want to look like a girl. I am not attracted to dudes (men). *If I look like a girl, I'm never going to get married,* I thought. Those were a rough couple of days for me emotionally. One day, I was using the bathroom, and I realized I still had manly features. Oh, happy day! "Celebrate good times, come on" I must say that was one of the happiest days of my life.

Anyway, I was on the oxygen for almost a week after I woke up. I hated that. I couldn't talk, I couldn't eat, and I couldn't drink. I also had double vision because one eye was pointing to the left and the other one straight ahead. I looked like the cuckoo bird in the Cocoa Puffs commercial. I was so thirsty, but I really couldn't drink anything. I also had a feeding tube in my stomach for nutrition. Still, I lost about twenty-five pounds during that time in Broward General Hospital. Jenny Craig didn't have anything on that diet plan, but it was way more expensiv

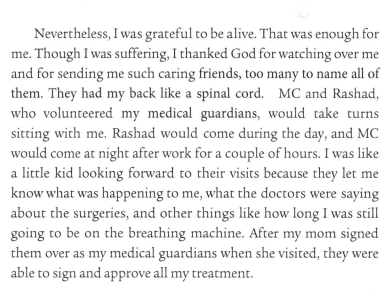

Nevertheless, I was grateful to be alive. That was enough for me. Though I was suffering, I thanked God for watching over me and for sending me such caring friends, too many to name all of them. They had my back like a spinal cord. MC and Rashad, who volunteered my medical guardians, would take turns sitting with me. Rashad would come during the day, and MC would come at night after work for a couple of hours. I was like a little kid looking forward to their visits because they let me know what was happening to me, what the doctors were saying about the surgeries, and other things like how long I was still going to be on the breathing machine. After my mom signed them over as my medical guardians when she visited, they were able to sign and approve all my treatment.

Dr. EB and Nadine would come on his lunch break and just sit and stare while I was in a coma. Many others came to visit me as well, including Skip, Daryl, Natasha, Randy, Kathy, JP, Joe, Rene, Marcello, Pastor Jym, Craig, Nicole, JC, Steve and Brenda Ramella, and so many others. I am forever grateful.

The doctors finally got high enough blood counts to perform the reconstructive facial surgery. After the surgery, they inserted a trachea tube in my throat to breathe and talk. I sounded like a robot, but at least I could talk. It was removed after a couple of days, and then I worked with a speech therapist to teach me how to swallow. I could finally drink something and, later, eat something. I was on a soft diet. Kathy Novak came and cut my chicken into itsy bitsy pieces and fed me. I hadn't noticed before because my jaw was wired shut, but I had lost my all of my bottom, except for the pair of backmost molars. No! Tell me it ain't so. That was heartbreaking to me. I always loved biting into a crisp, juicy apple. I didn't dwell on it, though. I had life, and that was what mattered. From what they told me, God had once again preserved my life! It was a surprise because when most people saw my head, they weren't sure I was going to make it.

During the three weeks I was in the intensive care unit, ninety-five percent of that time I was unconscious. After about three and a half weeks, they took me off some of the drugs, and I was finally placed in respite care. I still remember being told I couldn't use the bathroom without calling for help. Well, I have always been a stubborn guy who doesn't believe in the word "can't," so one day, I tried to go by myself. I almost did, but I still had double vision at that time. When I got to the bathroom door, I saw two door handles, so I played a game of "Eenie, Meenie, Minie, Moe." Needless to say, I picked the wrong handle, and when I reached for it, I fell flat on my face. Oops! Thankfully, the patient care technicians heard the commotion. When they arrived, I was lying in a pool of urine. Of course, at that moment, they weren't too happy with me because they had to clean me up. It's hard for a man to not be able to clean himself. In fact, I remember relieving and laying in it for at least an hour while I waited for someone to change me after doing #2. I don't wish that on anyone. It's like that saying: "Once a man, twice a child."

Eventually, I did become functional enough to be discharged, and I was transferred to an inpatient rehab clinic. HealthSouth Rehab Center in Sunrise, as it was the closest option. I think that was a good choice. At HealthSouth, the staff was very nice, and because the dietitian ate gluten-free, the menu had a lot of gluten-free options for me.

While I was there, I focused on the verse Colossians 3:23, which says, "Everything you do, do it as unto the Lord."

That verse and Philippians 4:19 drove my rehab. Every day, every session, every repetition, I tried to give 110 percent, even in the small things, like taking a step up the model steps or repeating sentences in speech therapy.

What I learned in my time at HealthSouth is Jesus never leaves our side. One morning, I was in so much pain from the surgery, and it was the weekend with no one visiting. I asked, "Where are you, Jesus?"

He sternly corrected me in the spirit. "I never left your side. While you were lazy and sleep in the coma, I was making sure that all your bills were paid, that countless people prayed for you, and most importantly that you kept breathing!"

After that, I hushed my mouth on that subject.

Everywhere I went in HealthSouth, I had to ride in a wheelchair. Again, I was supposed to call a nurse to help me go to the restroom, but remember, I'm quite stubborn. I had been doing well in therapy, so I figured I could make it from the wheelchair to the toilet by myself. I was correct in that assumption. I made it from the wheelchair to the toilet alright, but I got stuck on the toilet after handling my business. For the life of me, I couldn't lift my right foot off the ground, so I called the nurse to help me. Like the previous nurses, she wasn't happy with me for trying to do it by myself. However, when she told the doctor that I could not get my right foot off the ground, he sent me to get a CAT scan.

The next day, when I was in therapy, the nurse came to get me and said they had to rush me back to Broward General to have emergency surgery. She told me that I had a subdural hematoma, a brain bleed. On the way to the hospital, the nurses inserted a catheter in me, which worsened my pain even more. I don't know which is worse, getting a catheter inserted or taken out. Ouch!!!

During the surgery, they cut a hole in my skull to release the fluid pressure. Due to this, I now have a dent in my head and, of course, scars on my face, but that's cool with me because it gives me character.

Oddly enough, after that surgery, my speech became a lot clearer. I even began to walk better. I felt that I was close to normal. Well, I wasn't quite back to normal for good, but I felt I was making good progress.

After about four weeks in HealthSouth, Blue Cross Blue Shield notified me that they were not going to pay my bill anymore. When they got word of this news, the HealthSouth staff abruptly told me, "You don't have to go home, but you need to get out here."

So after two months in the hospital and rehab, I was finally going back home, or so I thought. HealthSouth could not release me without someone at home to watch out for me. When my brothers found this out, MC decided that I would stay with him at his home. Rashad would pick me up in the morning to go to therapy and drop me off at MC's after. That was a huge sacrifice for MC because he is a type-A person and very organized, and I am a type-B person and just the opposite. I'm laid-back and easygoing. He would buy food and not ask for anything back. On the weekends, I would go home and stay with my roommates to give MC a break from my disorganized habits.

I was prescribed seizure medication, Dilantin or "rat poison," that I was directed to take four times a day because of the brain bleed that I'd had. I considered all medicine to be "rat poison." Then, I stubbornly said, in classic Tray fashion, "Man, I never had a seizure. I don't need that medicine." I stopped taking the prescribed medication for about a week. During that time, I was still doing well in my therapy. I was staying focused on giving 110 percent for everything and every rep because whatever we do, we are to do it with all we got. Everything you do in life you need to give 100%

One day, JC took me to a doctor appointment at Broward General and then on to lunch at a place I loved: Whole Foods. When we were in the car on the way home, I had a spell where I was acting like I was drunk or high. I wanted to talk, but I was not cognitively clear; I was confused. John wanted to take me to the emergency room, but I refused and said I would be alright when I got home and was able to rest. I felt fine for a couple of days after that, until my next episode.

Then one day, MC was off work early, and he wanted to go out on his kayak. When he returned, I wanted to help, so I helped him pull his kayak out of the water. Then he went in front to open the garage, and that is all I remember about that day. Why? Because when MC came back, I had a blank look on my face, and I wasn't responding to him. Somehow, he was able to walk me into the house while he was calling 911. As we waited for an ambulance, I urinated on his couch, for that is one of the effects of seizures. That's a miracle that he still is my brother because he just got that couch.

Three days later, I woke up in Westside Regional Hospital, but the improvements I had gained from the last surgery had all regressed. "Where in the world am I." Rashad explained what happened. My speech and motor skills were most negatively affected. My speech was heavily slurred, I was drooling a lot more, and I started dragging my feet.

----

*That experience showed me that in life, we must
live and learn, especially from our mistakes.*

Sometimes, we must learn some hard lessons, and that was one of the hard ones for me. "Obedience is better than sacrifice" (1 Sam. 15:22). I should've taken that medicine to help my brain heal after experiencing that trauma instead of saying taking it meant a lack of faith. I am still experiencing some of the consequences of those lessons today. Maybe my speech would be a little clearer.

Nevertheless, it is important to never beat yourself up about it—don't dwell on your mistakes or regret them. You just need to try to take the lesson learned and "Dust yourself off and try again."² We need to "forget those things which are behind, and reaching forth unto those things which are before, press toward the mark for the prize." (Phil. 3:13-14 KJV). It is also important to remember to only play the hand you're dealt and enjoy the game. That is how I try to live my life.

So I continued to go to therapy for another one and a half months until one day, when I went home and checked the mail, when I received an unexpected letter. *Hmm, a letter from the AIDS Healthcare Foundation. What's this?* I wondered. The letter simply said that I would have to come back to work immediately or forfeit my position. Whoa! I wasn't ready for that at all. *What? I don't feel that I am physically ready,* I thought. Whether I felt I was ready or not, if a man doesn't work, he doesn't eat (2 Thess. 3:13). I like to eat, so I had to go to the lead doctor at the therapy center to ask for a letter permitting me to return to work.

---

² https://en.wikipedia.org/wiki/Try_Again_(Aaliyah_song)

I received the letter to go back to work, but when I first returned to the van, I just couldn't keep up with the demands. Dr. EB graciously allowed me to come and work with him in the office. He created a makeshift position just so I could get paid. After a couple of months, despite my gratitude for his kindness, I was eager to return to my original position because I never liked being inside and at a desk all day. Still, I was thankful because it was what I needed to adjust to being back in a work environment for eight hours a day.

After about six months of working in the AIDS Healthcare Foundation office, I asked to get back on the truck. As an HIV Testing Counselor, I would be expected to do HIV testing, engage in informative outreach within the community, and educate those at risk to ensure they were well-informed on how to protect themselves in the future. The HIV Testing Counselor also worked with the Public Health Department to coordinate local events. When I first went back on the truck, Dr. EB had my back again by letting me just do outreach to recruit clients for testing. Skip and Wilson would do all the hardwork, while I just did outreach. That's just the type of people they are. Skip would become my big brother. He always watched out for my wellbeing and sacrificed whatever for my health. He still does so. I was sick so often at that time we created the term Jordan-day. In the 1997 NBA Finals game, Michael Jordan played with a stomach virus. They won the game, but at the end of the game, Scottie Pippen had to help him walk off the court. Like Pippen to Jordan, Skipped helped me make it through the workday a countless number of times.

He would ask me, "Is it a Jordan-day?" or "Do you need to lay down?"

He could see my sickness, even though I would always try to hide it. Even though we don't see each other as much now, he can still hear it in my voice over the phone. I would use my lunch break time to lie down in the cab of the truck, instead of eating lunch. Thankfully, all of my coworkers allowed me to lie down when I was sick and drained. I would try my hardest to only take the thirty minutes allotted for our breaks and ask my coworkers to come and get me from the cab if I went over the time.

My time at the AIDS Healthcare Foundation was very humbling, especially after Dr. EB retired. Despite my education, I was the low man on the totem pole. Each day, I just focused on the verse, "Humble yourself before the Lord and He will lift you" (James 4:10 ESV). I knew that one day God would lift me up. Seven years after my accident, He definitely did; O' boy, he definitely did!

My Challenges Continue

Even though I was out of the hospital, my health was declining, I was noticeably losing weight, and my friends were concerned. I dropped down to 126 pounds. My face was sunken in, and I looked like a feeble, old man.

Now that I was back on the seizure medicine, I also went through a period of depression. It was medicine for the electric currents in my brain. So that was a side effect. I had always been an upbeat, silly person, but I was more like Eeyore from Winnie the Pooh when I was on the seizure medication. "Well, I guess I better eat something. It's just food."

Thankfully, my friends helped me through this period. It touches my heart to think about how my friends helped love me back to health during that time of my life. I couldn't drive because of my seizure history. Steve and Diane Robles took me to and from my doctor appointments. Steve picked me up for the Refuge and then took me to Boston Market. Steve Ramella and

Joe Iocovozzi, my roommate and great friend, had breakfast with me every week, even when I wasn't too social. Steve, Brenda, Joe, and Lianda continued to love me despite my depressing mood. My two roommates, Rene Staeldi and Joe, took me grocery shopping as well. Joe is like my brother from an Italian mother. He was selfless and would do whatever I needed, including providing me with rides and cooked meals. I mean, he would do whatever. Once or twice, I lost control of my bowels in the kitchen. He saw it on the floor and didn't talk bad about me; he just cleaned it up, and I heard nothing else about it. I still make an annual trip to visit him, his wonderful wife, Lianda, and his two adorable kids, Liliana and Liam. I am so thankful for all the rides I was given because after my seizure, I was very fearful of having that experience on a bus or at a bus stop. There go that scaredy cat again.

Further, there were some other difficulties my friends also helped me overcome as well. I missed one of my rheumatologist appointments because I simply forgot about it. I was just trying to keep my head above water. I was still very sick and weak, but I needed to work and make a living. At times, it was quite overwhelming. I wasn't the best at keeping my appointments, so when I went back to my rheumatologist, she was so frustrated with me missing my appointment and not hearing from me for a month that she dropped me as a client. I remember that like it was yesterday. When I got in the car after that appointment, I began to cry.

Yeah, that is right. As a thirty-three-year-old man, I was crying. There were just so many emotions with my health, work, and now my doctor's dismissal all at once—I was broken to the core. If you ever saw the movie *Friday*, there is a scene in which Craig, played by Ice Cube, gets fired from his job on his day off, and his dad says, "Craig, how do you get fired on your day off." Well, then I said to myself, "Tray, how do you get fired by your doctor. You are the epitome of non-compliant."

Then, Diane Robles said something that blessed me: "Let's just press RESET. I'm going to help you with remembering, getting to your appointments, and also back to looking healthy."

I am humbled when I think about her act of love, as well as all the others that helped me through this challenging time in my journey. Each week, Monique would bring me a pot of soup because she was worried about my weight. For four years, I could not bite into an apple because I could only gum food after losing so many teeth. Imagine a 33 year old guy needing dentures.

As I got stronger, I was finally able to keep up with everyone with HIV testing. It was also time for me to be allowed to drive again. I saved enough money to buy a car off Craigslist. I believe it was a silver 2009 Hyundai Elantra, which had a nice interior and a pretty good stereo. I was on the road again. I enjoyed my car for about a week, but in classic Tray form, on my way to a farmer's market to get apples—go figure—in North Lauderdale, I was crossing an intersection when—bam! I was sideswiped by another car on the driver's side. The car was totaled. The medic had to pull me out through the passenger's side.

I was in excruciating pain on my side and back. I was taken to the emergency room, where the doctors checked me out. It was a miracle that nothing was broken. I just had some bruised ribs. Now, I had to find another car. I wish it would have been that easy, but the emergency room doctor reported to the Florida Department of Highway Safety and Motor Vehicles that she didn't feel I was medically able to drive because of my speech. You know, discrimination happens to many people, and it does to uniquely-abled people as well. I assume she probably thought that I was cognitively unable to drive because of the way I talked.

To anyone else who has experienced this, please don't get down on yourself. You are a phenomenal person. You are wonderfully made just as God planned (Psalm 139:14). You are marvelous in His sight (Zech. 2:8). He knows your true ability is in Him and His ability through you.

So I had to go through a medical review with the DMV. This was not an overnight deal at all. I had to see several doctors, fill out applications, and wait and wait and wait! Yet, I had to continue to get to work. God has always faithfully provided for me though. He provided me with Dr. EB. You see, I moved into his neighborhood just a week before the accident. Now that I didn't have a car, he would drop his daughter off at school and then return home, a full seven miles out of his way, in rush-hour traffic to pick me up for work. Skip and Wilson, my coworkers, would graciously take me home after work. I don't know how many times I heard Skip say, "Do you need me to take you home?" Skip even took me home after a night shift ended at three in the morning, even though I lived thirty minutes away from him.

That is true unconditional love. During this time of being unable to drive, I felt so isolated. I couldn't go anywhere but work and church. Usually, I'm a social butterfly, but now I lived by myself, so I felt lonely. This period made me even more appreciative of my relationships with friends and family so much more.

To anyone who feels alone because of your differences, just know you are never alone. Conversely, to anyone with relation-ships, treasure those relationships. Over that year, I only had to take the bus to work about five times. That's amazing, considering I worked full-time and went to church twice a week.

After a year of waiting and riding my squealing bike like "Deebo" to get groceries, I finally got approved to take the driver's license written and road tests. Yes, that's right. I had to take my driver's license test again and pass it like I was sixteen years old again. I had to pass the road test three times in a row. That was no problem; driving is like riding a bike. You never forget how to drive. Praise God, I passed!

During this time, Rashad died. I cannot remember ever crying so much. God had to have a two-gallon bottle to collect those tears. I did not sleep for a week. He was and will always indeed be my blood brother. Just two months after this, my grandfather died. What?! Two men I greatly look up to as real men. I was crushed!

As time went on, I slowly but surely gained some weight back. All the while I was still working at the AIDS Healthcare Foundation. I even started jogging, which was really a quick limp. I was able to get dental implants to replace those teeth I lost in the bike accident. I needed almost my entire row of bottom teeth, except my two back molars, replaced. It took about four years because I had to get two to three bone grafts and wait six months each to see if my body accepted them. I had countless dentist appointments. Finally, I was back to being an apple addict, and it helped my speech and appearance as well.

Pause for Reflection...

As you followed my life's journey in this chapter, you may have related to my frustration as challenges and obstacles continually arose before me. Each time, though, God was there with me. That told me God still had work for me to do here on the earth.

Have you had experiences that assure you God is with you and has a purpose for you here on the earth?

As you read, we have to live and learn—especially from our mistakes. I also learned it is important to never beat yourself up about it, dwell on your mistakes, or regret them. You just need to try to take the lesson learned and do like Aaliyah said: "Dust yourself off and try again."

Take the time to review the scriptures that helped me through the challenges and obstacles I faced during this part of my journey. Also, remember to be thankful for the people God has put in your life to help and guide you.

Philippians 4:18-19

Philippians 4:13-14

Colossians 3:23

Philippians 3:13

James 4:10

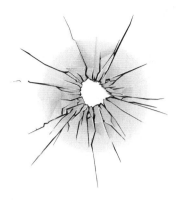

CONCLUSION

God Is Consistent

The one consistent thing in my life has been
Jesus riding these challenges out with me.

In my journey, I made some mistakes. I learned to give my all in everything I do, every single day, and to let the chips fall where they may. I may not be quick or efficient at what I do, but to each my pillow, I can lay, knowing I did my best. I have also learned not to "try to keep up with the Joneses" because the Joneses have their own story, and I have mine. Only God gets the glory, and it only matters what He thinks of our efforts. It is lovely to know that the Lord does not see as man sees, "for man looks at the outward appearance, but the Lord looks at the heart" (1 Sam. 16:7).

From my story, I hope you have learned you are special to God. You are the apple of His eye (Psalms 17:8). Please know that you are never alone. Jesus is with you. If God puts a goal or dream in you, go for it with all you have; don't lose faith in that dream. It just might come true. One thing I know is that no one can be an island. You need others. Finally, cherish your friends and family. Don't take your health or your friends and family for granted. You need them both more than you know.

Now, I am doing well. I bought a nice car, and I even bought my first home in a nice neighborhood! Remember that room I rented in which I had tears of sadness from sleeping on the floor? The first week in my new home, before my furniture arrived, I had tears of joy as I willingly slept on the floor. Things came full circle. Those student loans are paid off. I'm no longer at the AIDS Healthcare Foundation, but I am so thankful for the years I spent there.

As I am finishing this, the world is going through the coronavirus pandemic, but I'm not worried because Jesus is riding this all out with me.

You cannot do this thing called life alone. Please, do not isolate yourself if you feel insecure because of your condition or your differences. Take comfort in that everyone is different in some way, some more than others. Cherish your friends and family. Each day, play the hand you are dealt and enjoy the game because if you give your best effort, then you win in God's eyes.

I just want to let you know that throughout your life, you are guaranteed to have ups, downs, and so-called bad hands, but rest assured, Jesus will walk it all out with you—if you let Him.

Jesus said in Matthew 28:20, "I am with you always, even unto the end of the world" (KJV).

If you have a love one who is uniquely-abled, I promise you they are very appreciative of your love and support. I have been blessed, as you've just read, with countless people who showed this to me. This makes me the richest person north of the equator.

My story is far from over. I still have so much more learning, growing, grinding, traveling, and dreaming to do. I may have faced a lot of adversity in my years, but that was all to make me better. God chose to use this little old, pigeon-toed soldier as a vessel of love for those around me now and those I will meet in the future. Like a cockroach that got stepped on and consequently has a wing or a leg impaired, I'm still crawling around greatly enjoying this game called life. That being said, your story is not finished. He got you. Please always remember to be thankful in the good times and hopeful in the bad. Keep going! Keep loving! Keep the Faith!!

Acknowledgements

I want to first give a special thanks to Jesus because without You, I would not still be alive today.

Secondly, I want to thank my mom for giving me a love that only a mother can give. Miss you mom.

Thank you, Pastor Roberson, Brother and Sister Randall, Brother and Sister Pullen, and the rest of the KL family, for helping to nurture me through my college years.

Thank you, Kevin (Kevo) Kerns, for always being real and showing me that genuine love.

Thanks, Jeff Cook, for being there for me through a very rough period physically.

Thanks, Monique Bernier, for still loving me like your little brother.

Thanks, Daryl and Tasha Byrd, for continuing walk in life together with me. Likewise to you, Ramon and Debbie Hunley, John and Debbie Chambers, Akee and Lisa Campbell.

Thanks, Pastor Darren and Christine Bennett, for loving me like family. "Let me hear you say, Jesus!"

Thanks, Skip Saucier, for still being the big brother to me who will lovingly expect the best out of me but always there to help me when I fall short.

Thanks, Linda and Raymond Schwartz (Lay Lay and Ray Ray), Michele, Mike, Jamila, and the rest of the family, for adopting me.

Thanks, Dr. EB, Nadine, Ethan, and Asha, for your daily, unconditional love and support.

Thanks Pastor Steve Williams for being a mentor to many!

Matt and Hollie (MC and Lele), even though you are my little brother and sister in age, it's like you are my big brother and sister. Always watching out

Thanks, Steve and Brenda, for inviting me into your life as if you had known me forever.

Thanks, Julie Ferguson, for inspiring me to write this book. You always have an encouraging word for me.

Thanks, Ameena Shaheed (Mom), for raising Rashad to be the man that he became.

Thank you to Gloria Greenfield for assisting me during the writing process of this book.

In closing, Yay, yay, yay!!!!!

–Tray Williams

Made in the USA
Columbia, SC
24 June 2021

40978160R00057